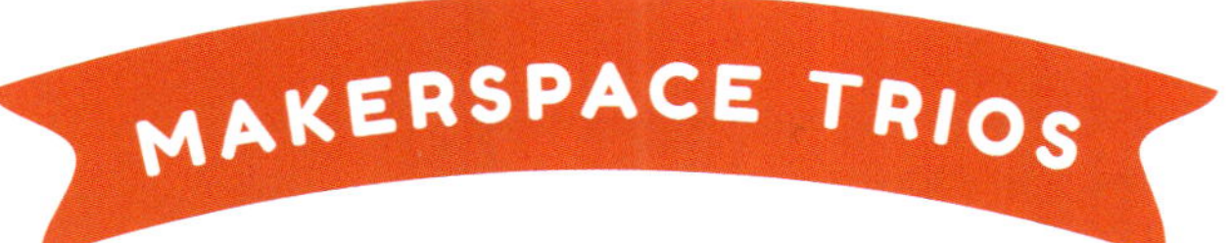

Creating with NEWSPAPER, BUTTONS & PAPER CLIPS

Rebecca Felix

Consulting Editor, Diane Craig,
M.A./Reading Specialist

Super Sandcastle

An Imprint of Abdo Publishing
abdobooks.com

abdobooks.com

Published by Abdo Publishing, a division of ABDO, PO Box 398166, Minneapolis, Minnesota 55439.

Printed in the United States of America, North Mankato, Minnesota
102021
012022

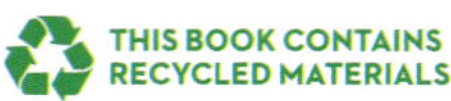

Design: Sarah DeYoung, Mighty Media, Inc.
Production: Mighty Media, Inc.
Editor: Megan Borgert-Spaniol
Cover Photographs: iStockphoto; Mighty Media, Inc.; Shutterstock Images
Interior Photographs: iStockphoto; Mighty Media, Inc.; Rene Passet/Flickr; SEMYON DANILOV/AP Images; Shutterstock Images

The following manufacturers/names appearing in this book are trademarks: Decomposition Book®, Elmer's®, Sharpie®

Library of Congress Control Number: 2021943029

Publisher's Cataloging-in-Publication Data

Names: Felix, Rebecca, author.
Title: Creating with newspaper, buttons & paper clips / by Rebecca Felix
Description: Minneapolis, Minnesota : Abdo Publishing, 2022 | Series: Makerspace trios | Includes online resources and index.
Identifiers: ISBN 9781532196447 (lib. bdg.) | ISBN 9781098218256 (ebook)
Subjects: LCSH: Handicraft--Juvenile literature. | Creative thinking--Juvenile literature.| Newspapers in art--Juvenile literature. | Buttons in art--Juvenile literature. | Paper clips--Juvenile literature. | Mixed Media crafts--Juvenile literature.
Classification: DDC 745.5--dc23

Super SandCastle™ books are created by a team of professional educators, reading specialists, and content developers around five essential components—phonemic awareness, phonics, vocabulary, text comprehension, and fluency—to assist young readers as they develop reading skills and strategies and increase their general knowledge. All books are written, reviewed, and leveled for guided reading and early reading intervention programs for use in shared, guided, and independent reading and writing activities to support a balanced approach to literacy instruction.

TO ADULT HELPERS

The projects in this book are fun and simple. There are just a few things to remember to keep kids safe. Some projects may use sharp or hot objects. Also, kids may be using messy supplies. Make sure they protect their clothes and work surfaces. Be ready to offer guidance during brainstorming and assist when necessary.

CONTENTS

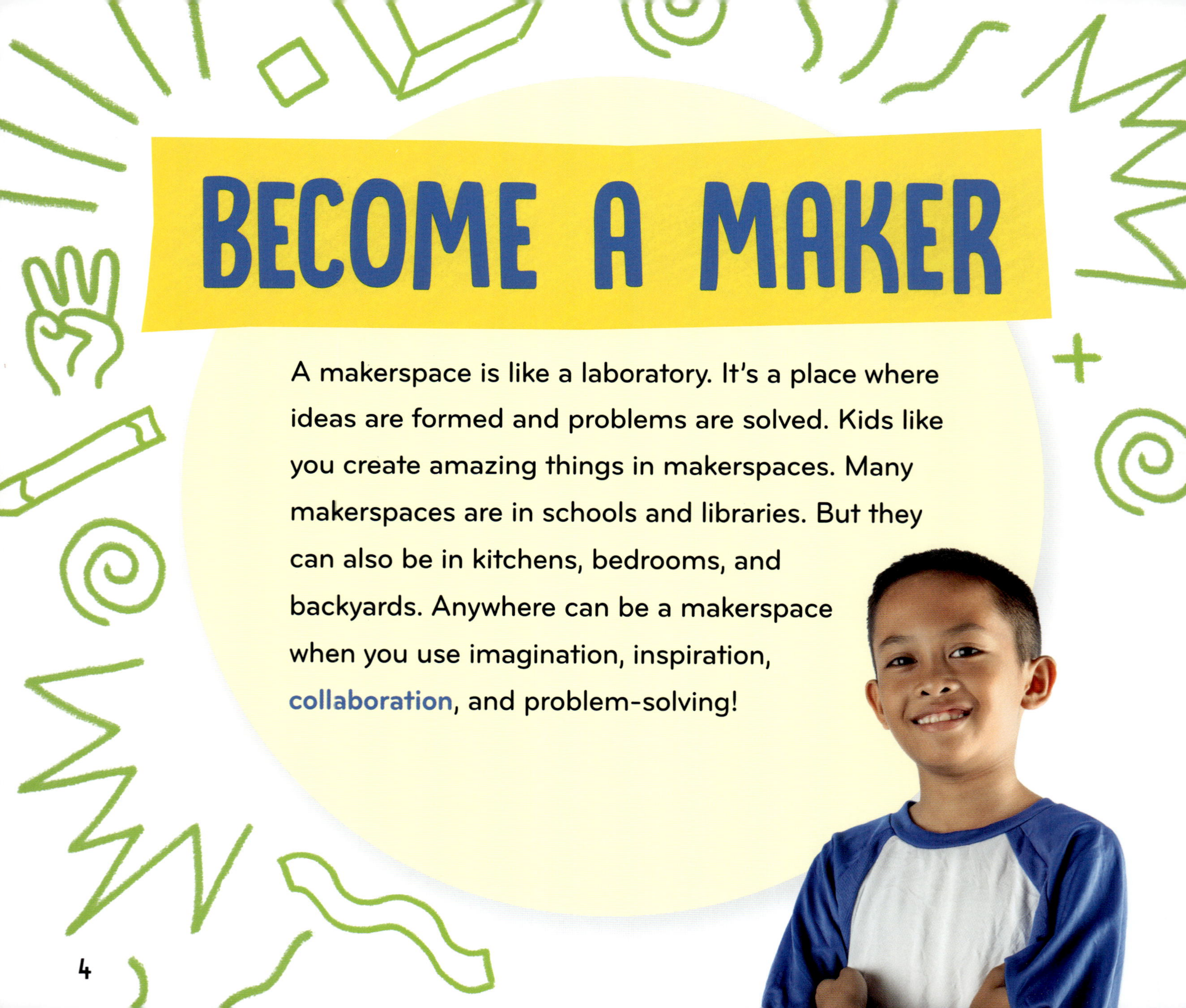

BECOME A MAKER

A makerspace is like a laboratory. It's a place where ideas are formed and problems are solved. Kids like you create amazing things in makerspaces. Many makerspaces are in schools and libraries. But they can also be in kitchens, bedrooms, and backyards. Anywhere can be a makerspace when you use imagination, inspiration, **collaboration**, and problem-solving!

Makerspace Toolbox

Imagination

This takes you to new places and lets you experience new things. Anything is possible with imagination!

Inspiration

This is the spark that gives you an idea. Inspiration can come from almost anywhere!

Collaboration

Makers work together. They ask questions and get ideas from everyone around them. Collaboration solves problems that seem impossible.

Problem-Solving

Things often don't go as planned when you're creating. But that's part of the fun! Find creative solutions to any problem that comes up. These will make your project even better.

EXPLORE NEWSPAPER

You probably come across a newspaper every week. This paper is made of wood **pulp**. It is used to print words and images in ink. Old newspaper is recycled or reused. People use it as a packing material, campfire starter, surface protector, and much more!

Newspaper Properties

- Easy to shape
- Foldable
- Lightweight
- Thin

How Can You Use Newspaper?

Newspaper has many standard uses. But it can be used however you like in a makerspace! Let your imagination wander. What would it look like to use newspaper in a new way?

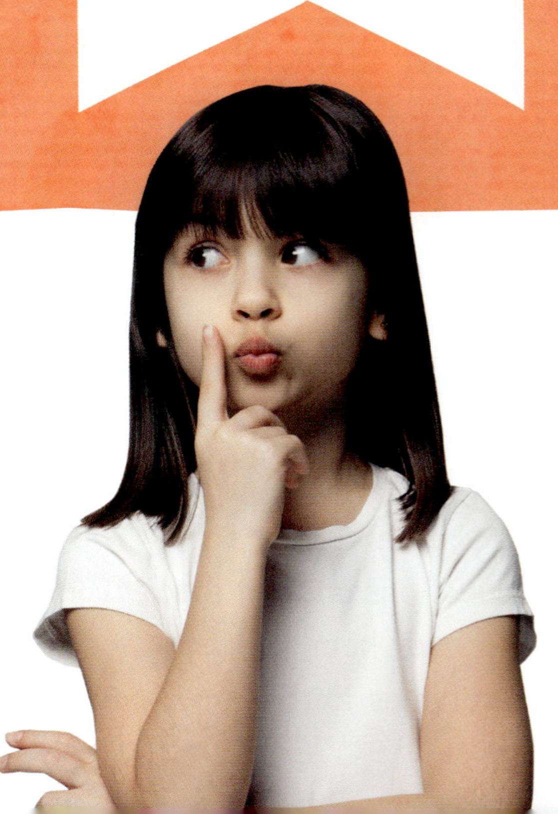

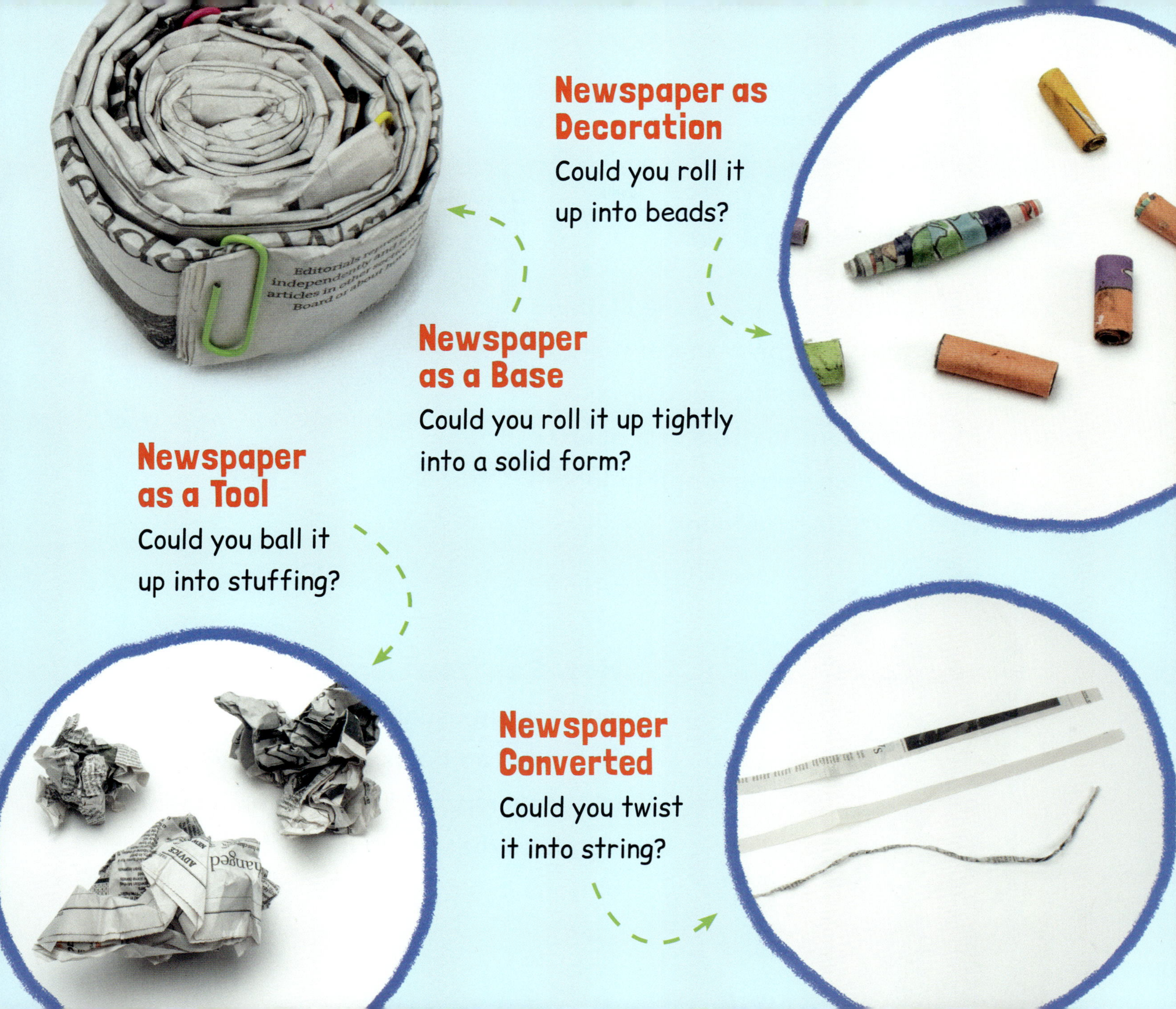

Newspaper as Decoration

Could you roll it up into beads?

Newspaper as a Base

Could you roll it up tightly into a solid form?

Newspaper as a Tool

Could you ball it up into stuffing?

Newspaper Converted

Could you twist it into string?

EXPLORE BUTTONS

Do you have buttons on any of the clothing you wear? Buttons can be made of many materials, including plastic, wood, and metal. Most are about the size of a quarter or smaller. They hold fabric together in shirts, pants, pockets, and more.

Button Properties

- Hard
- Holey
- Lightweight
- Round

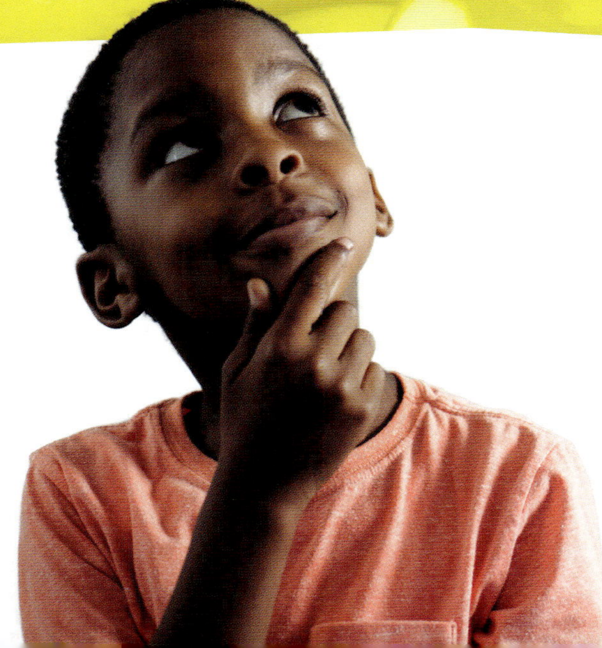

How Can You Use Buttons?

Buttons are usually used with clothing. But they can be used however you like in a makerspace! Let your imagination wander. What would it look like to use buttons in a new way?

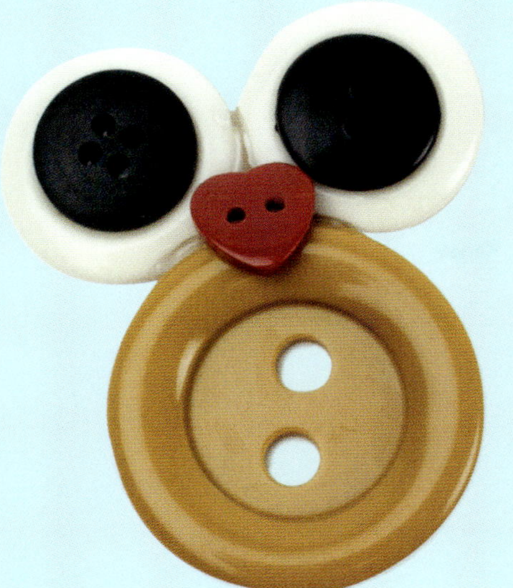

Buttons as a Base

Could you glue them into a shape?

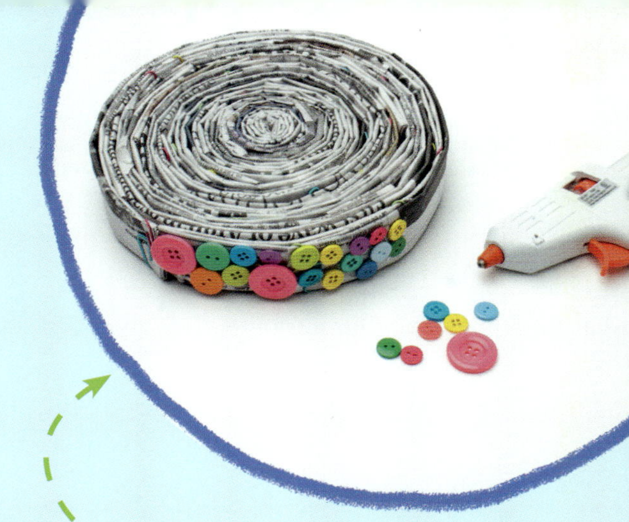

Buttons as Decoration

Could you use them to make eyes, ears, or polka dots?

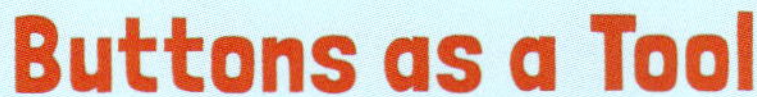

Buttons as a Tool

Could you trace them to make perfect circles?

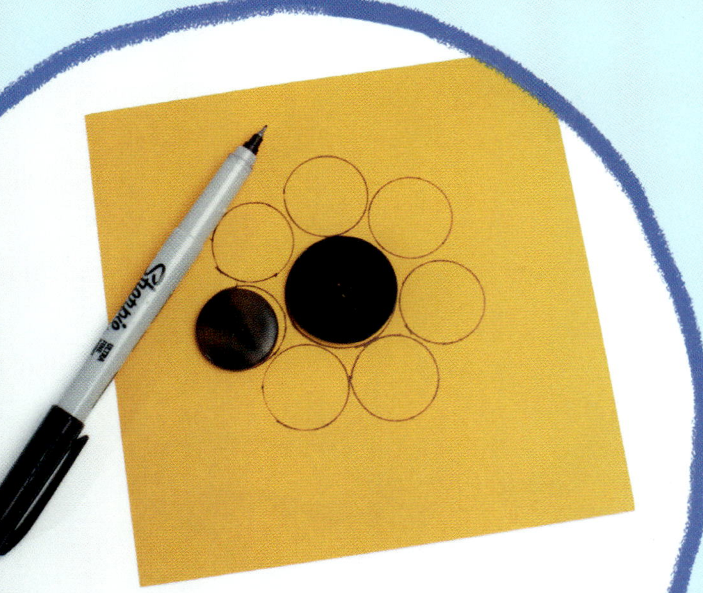

Buttons Converted

Could you stack them into a solid figure?

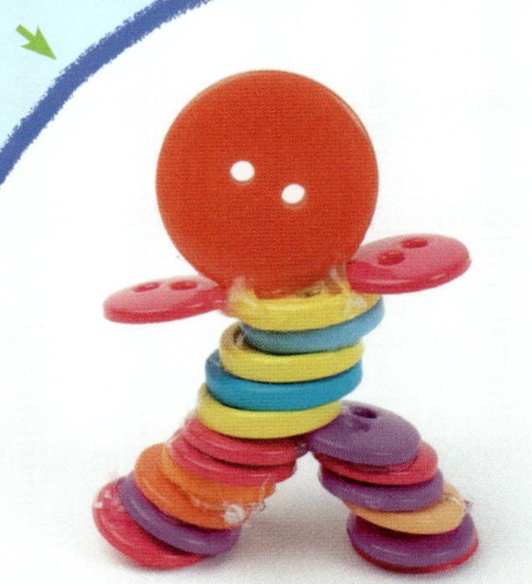

EXPLORE PAPER CLIPS

Paper clips are often made of metal. They can also be plastic. Paper clips come in many colors, shapes, and sizes. But they all have the same primary purpose. They are made to hold sheets of paper together!

Paper Clip Properties

- Bendable
- Lightweight
- Stiff
- Strong grip

How Can You Use Paper Clips?

Paper clips are often used with paper. But they can be used however you like in a makerspace! Let your imagination wander. What would it look like to use paper clips in a new way?

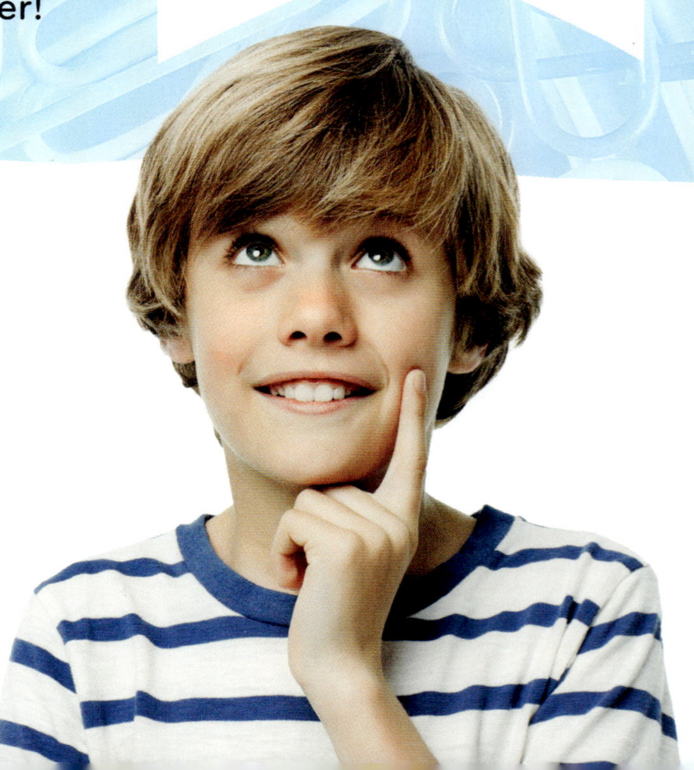

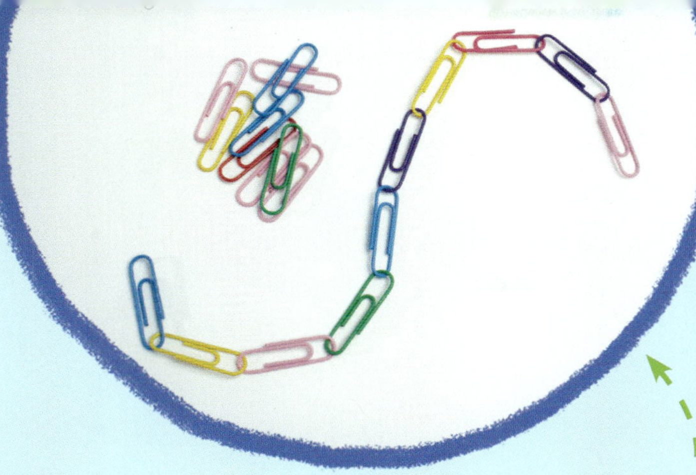

Paper Clips as Decoration

Could you use them to make hair, spikes, or wings?

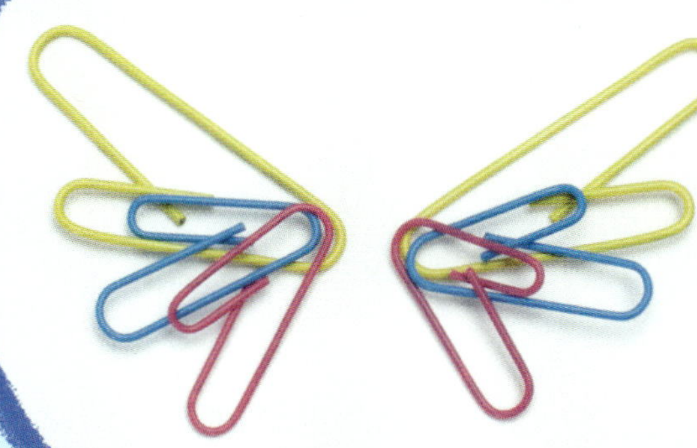

Paper Clips as a Base

Could you connect many of them to form a chain?

Paper Clips Converted

Could you straighten them and use them as wires?

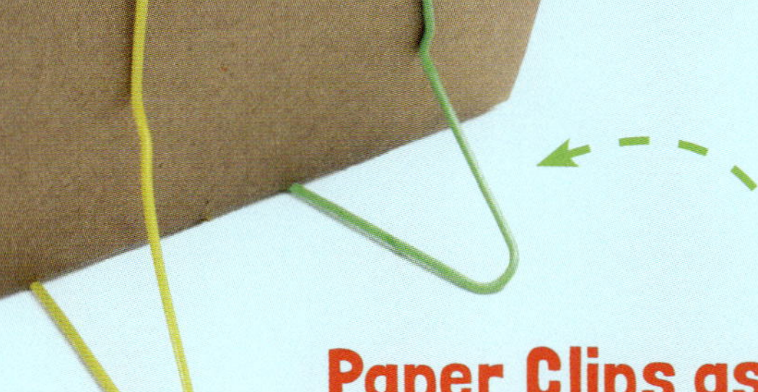

Paper Clips as a Tool

Could you use them to prop something up?

GET INSPIRED

People have used newspaper, buttons, and paper clips in all kinds of creative ways. Let these examples spark your imagination!

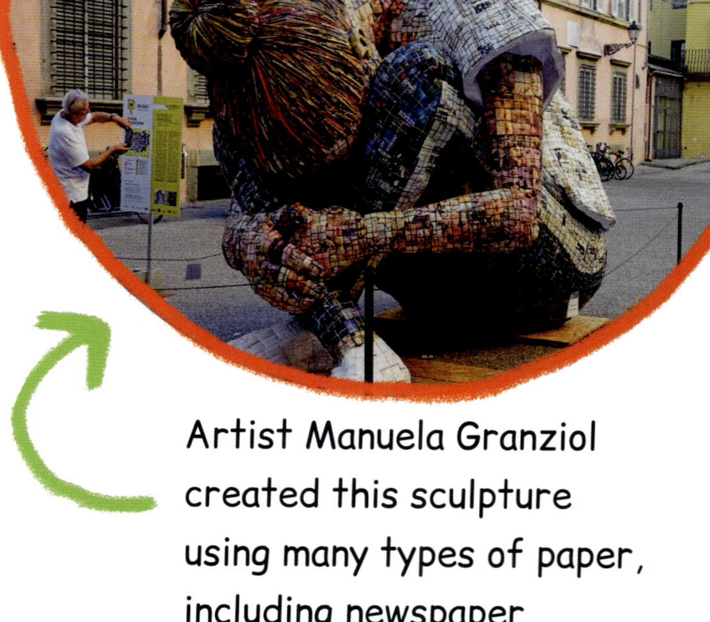

Artist Manuela Granziol created this sculpture using many types of paper, including newspaper.

Craftspeople in India create statues using newspaper.

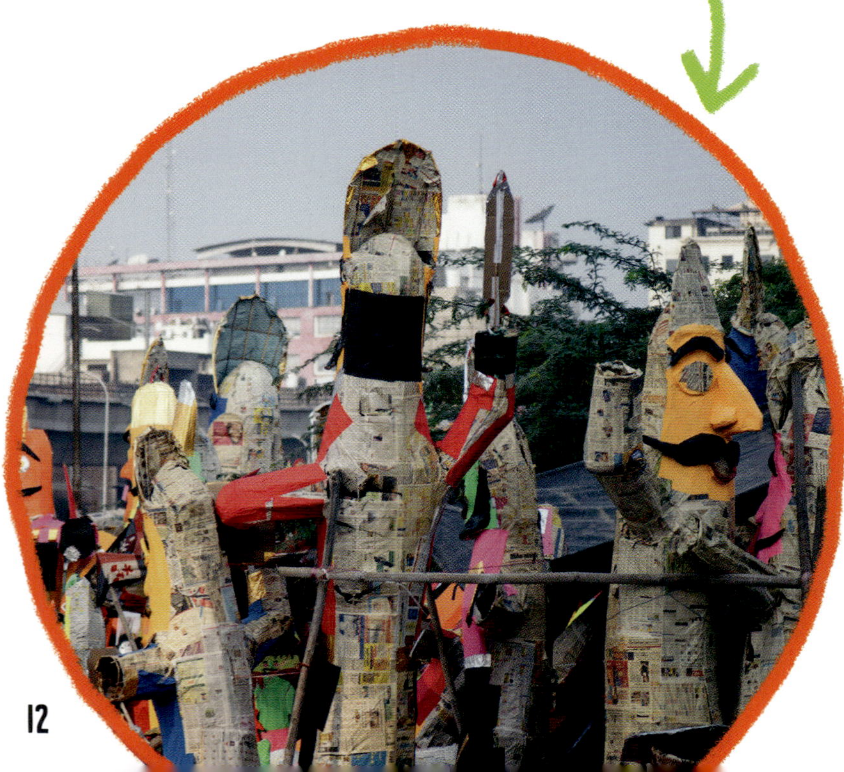

How could you bend and shape paper clips to give them life?

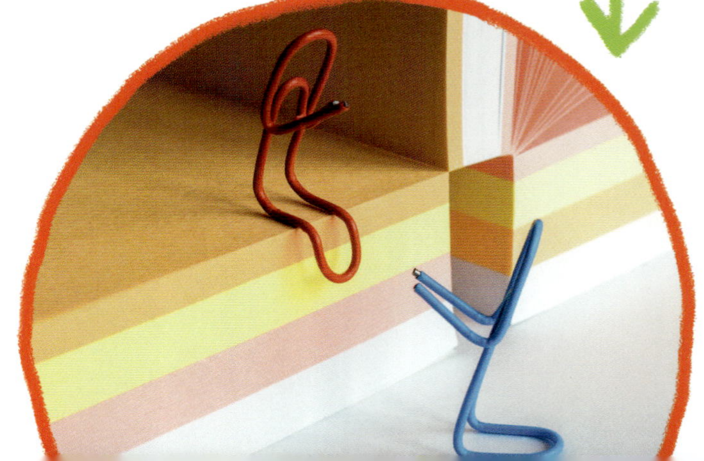

What kinds of objects can buttons represent?

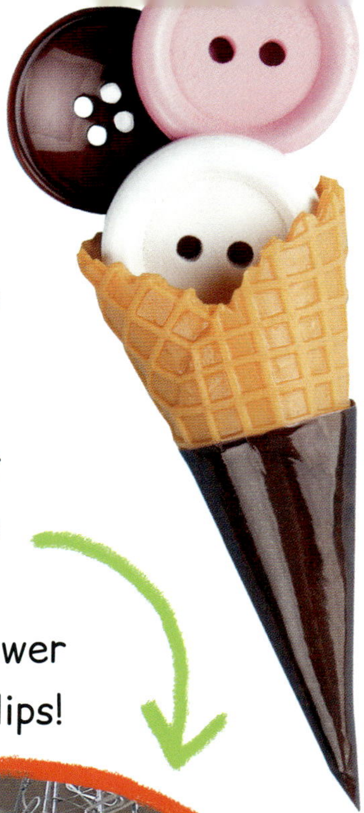

In Russia, student Elvira Timoshenko made a model of France's Eiffel Tower using 786 paper clips!

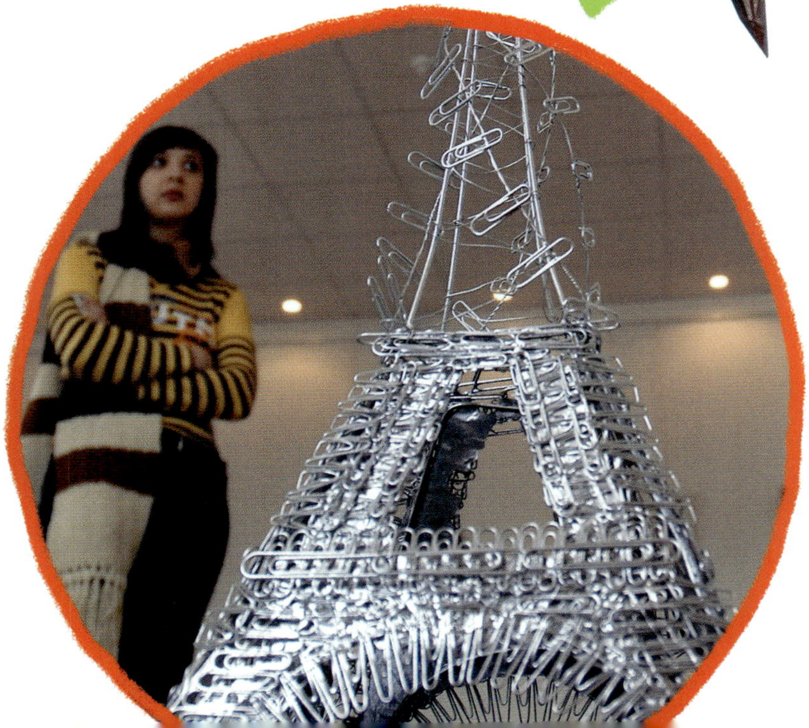

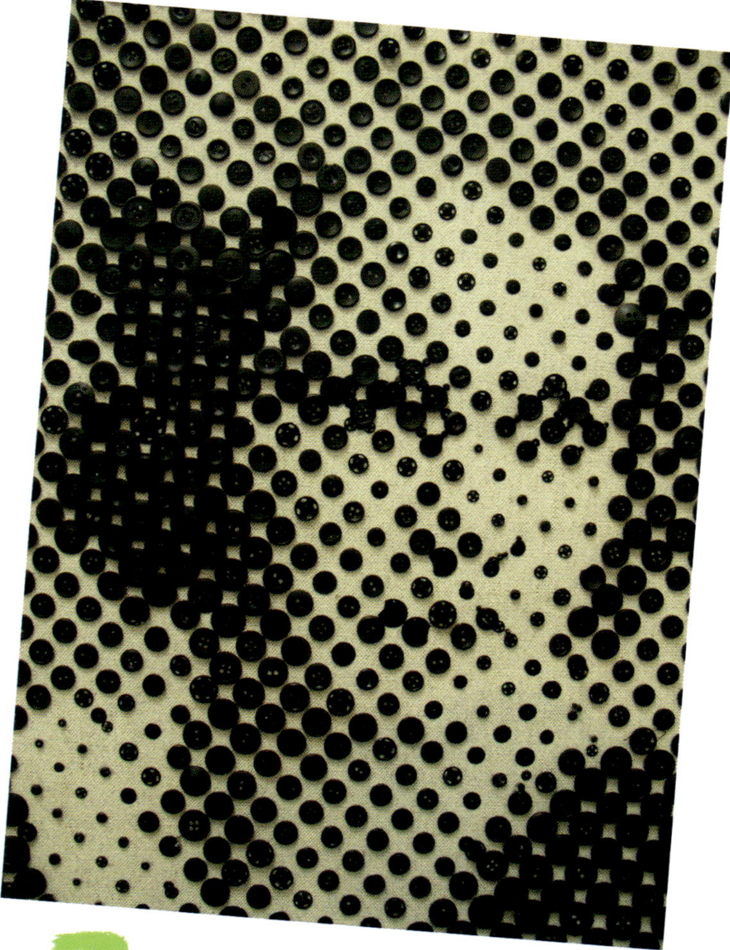

Can you see a woman's face in this button artwork?

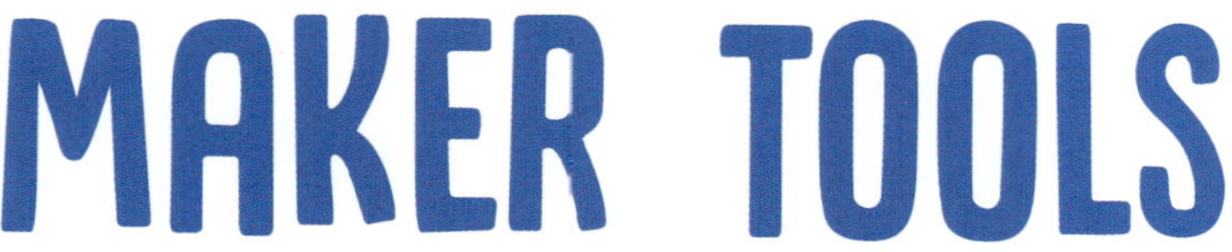

MAKER TOOLS

Are you inspired? Have you brainstormed some makerspace projects? It's time to gather your newspaper, buttons, and paper clips. You may also need a few everyday tools to cut and connect your primary materials.

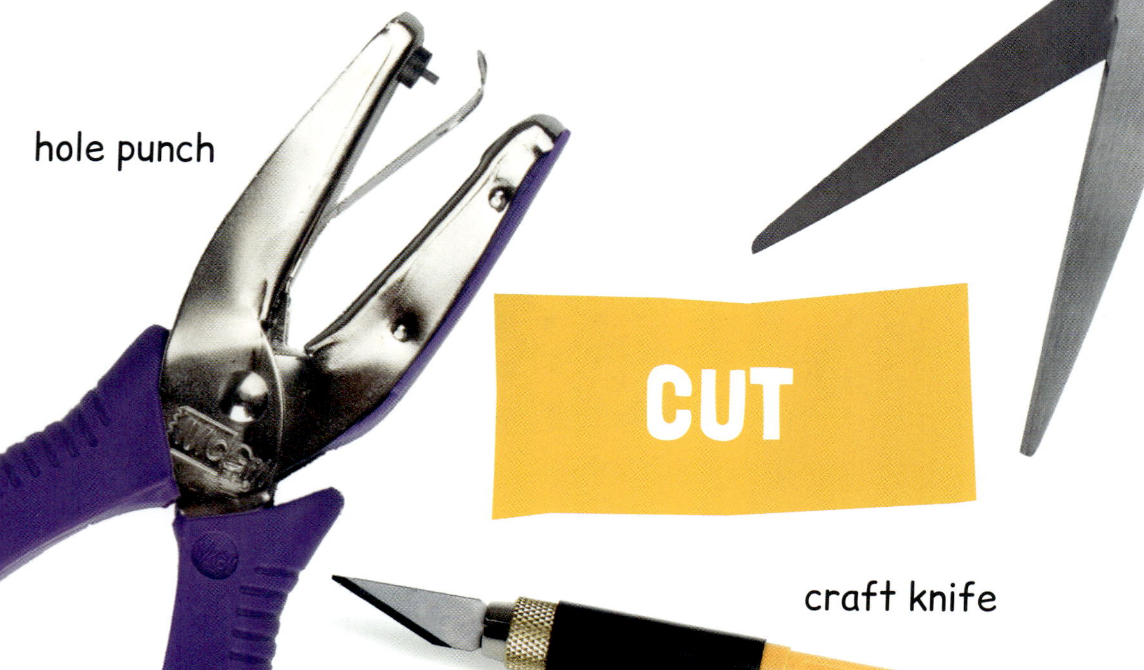

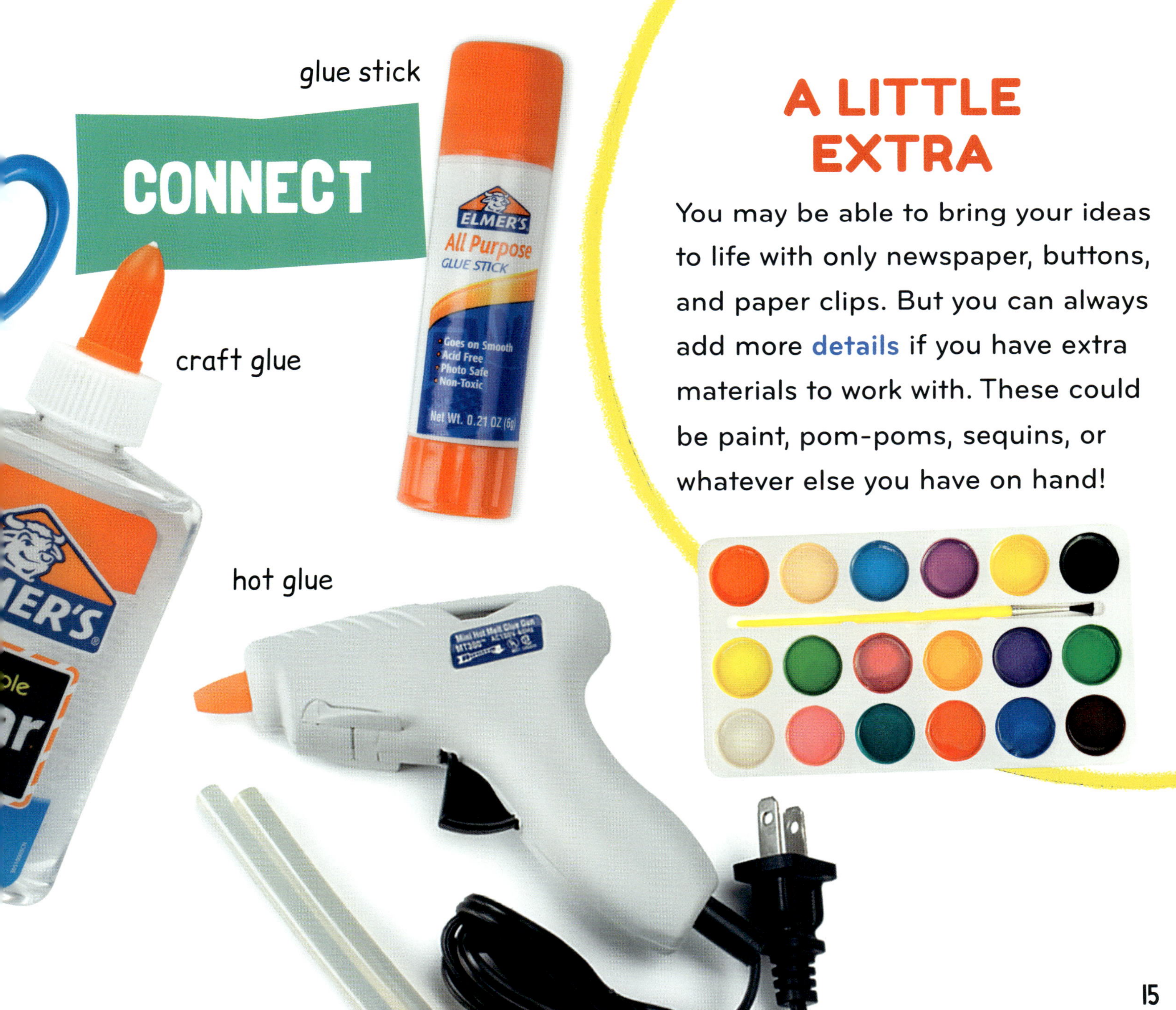

A LITTLE EXTRA

You may be able to bring your ideas to life with only newspaper, buttons, and paper clips. But you can always add more **details** if you have extra materials to work with. These could be paint, pom-poms, sequins, or whatever else you have on hand!

MAKING YOUR MAKERSPACE

You can let your imagination run wild in a makerspace. But be sure to follow these rules to stay safe and be respectful.

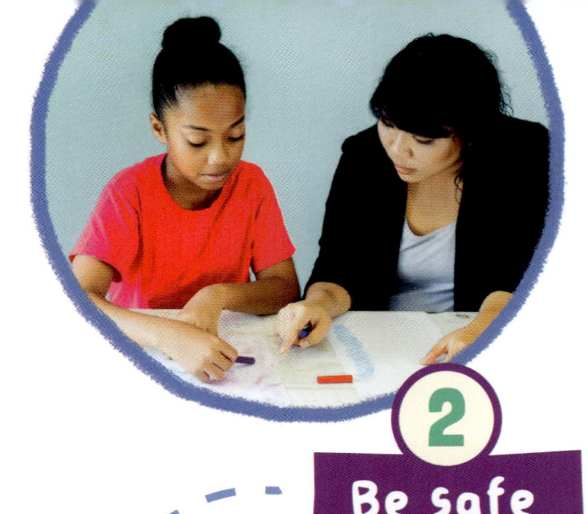

2 Be safe

Ask an adult for help when using sharp or hot tools, such as craft knives or glue guns.

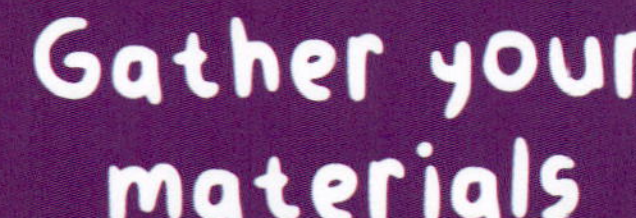

1 Gather your materials

Make sure an adult says it's OK to use what you gather.

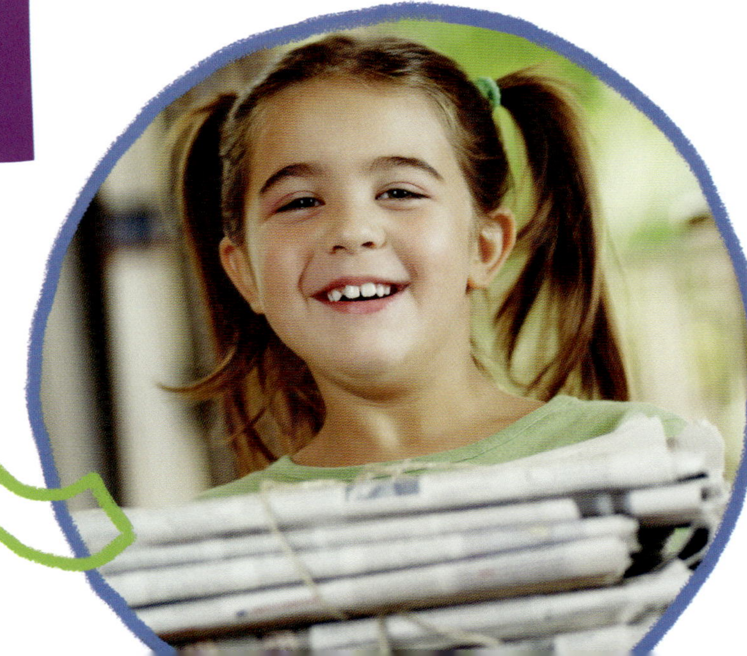

Share the space

Share supplies and space with other makers. You can invite them to share their ideas if you're feeling stuck!

4 Keep trying

Don't give up when things don't go exactly as planned. Instead, think about the problem you are having. What are some ways to solve it?

Clean up

Put away materials. Find a safe space to store unfinished projects until next time. And clean up any scraps, spills, or messes you made.

DISPLAY IT

Create an artwork from newspaper, buttons, and paper clips. Then put it on display!

Tightly roll up sheets of newspaper and secure them with glue.

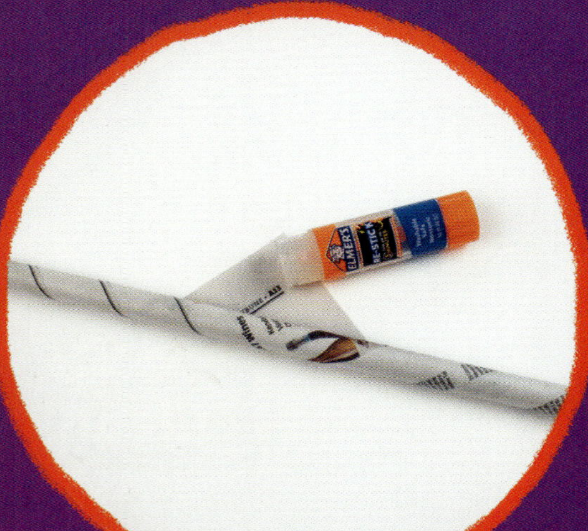

Glue together buttons to make a cute critter. Make wings and feathers out of paper clips!

Paint the newspaper rolls to look like trees. Glue them together to create a canvas.

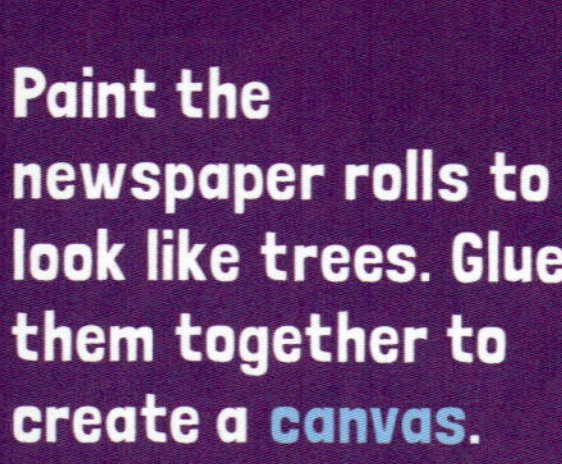

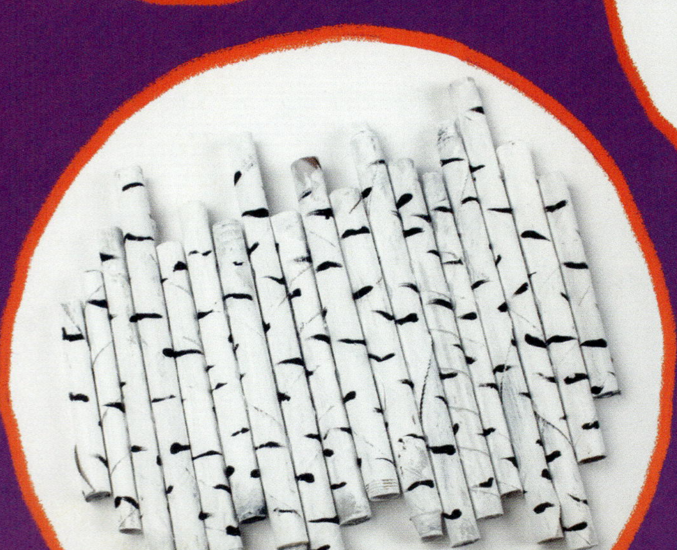

Unwind paper clips and hook them together to make a hanger.

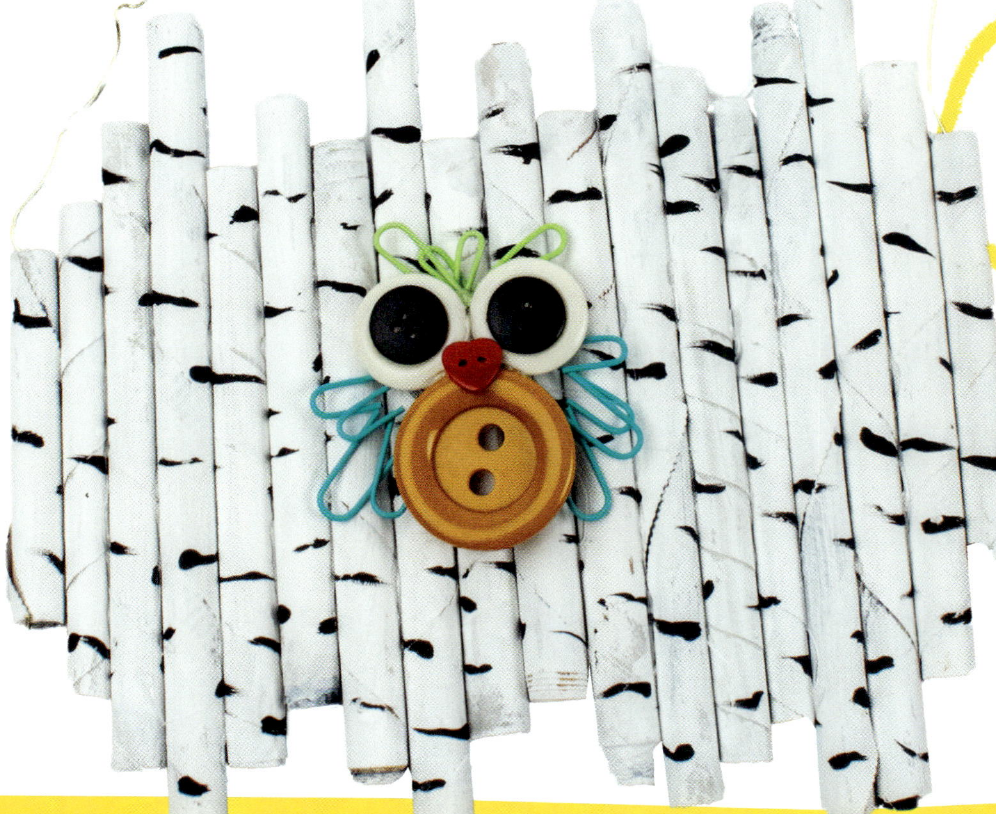

Imagine

Imagine ideas with no limits. Could you make a newspaper artwork to cover an entire wall? Or bend a single paper clip into a tiny sculpture?

Your Turn!

Could you make a desktop sculpture using only newspaper and glue?

Could you sketch a scene and then color it in with buttons?

How could you use paper clips to hang or **prop** up your artwork?

WEAR IT

What wearable clothing or accessories could you make from newspaper, buttons, and paper clips?

Weave together strips of newspaper.

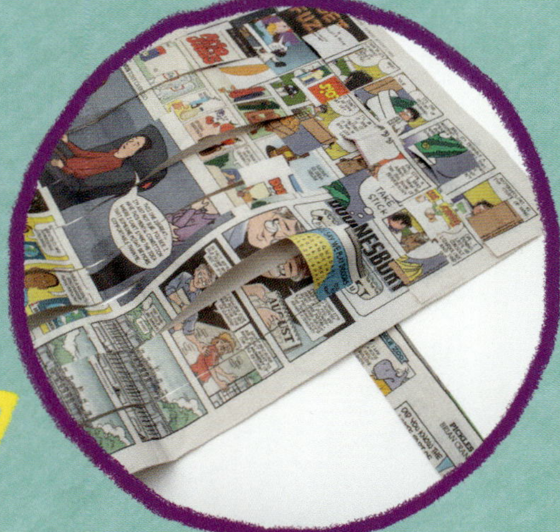

Fold up your newspaper fabric and secure the sides with paper clips.

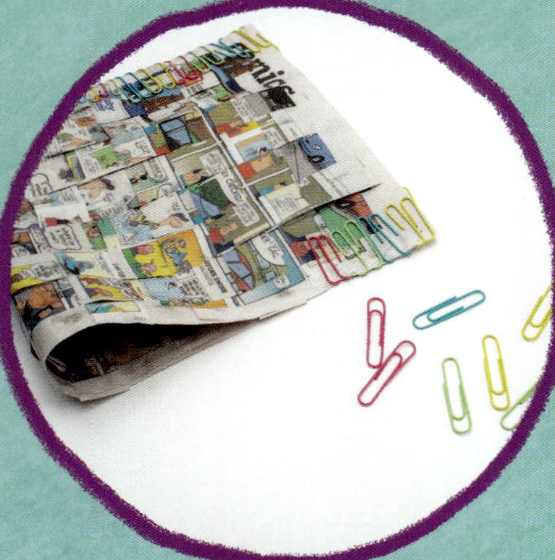

Brush a layer of glue onto the newspaper to make it more durable.

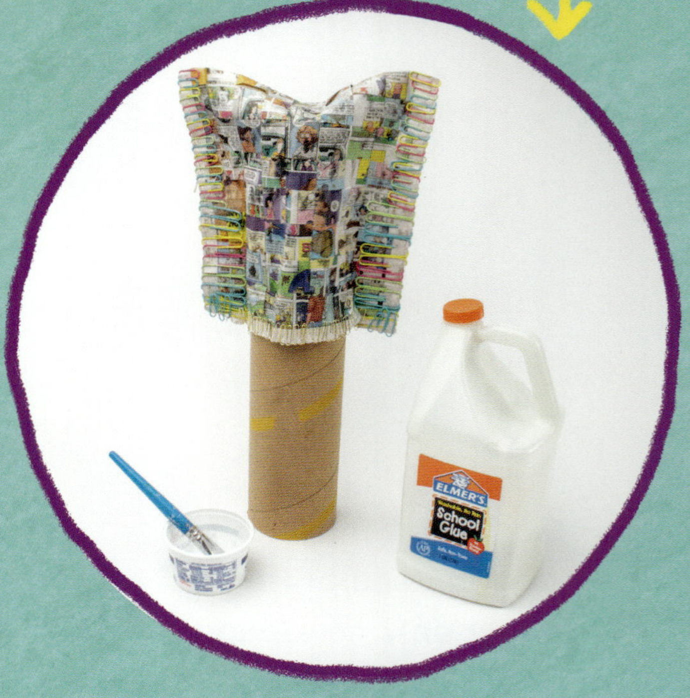

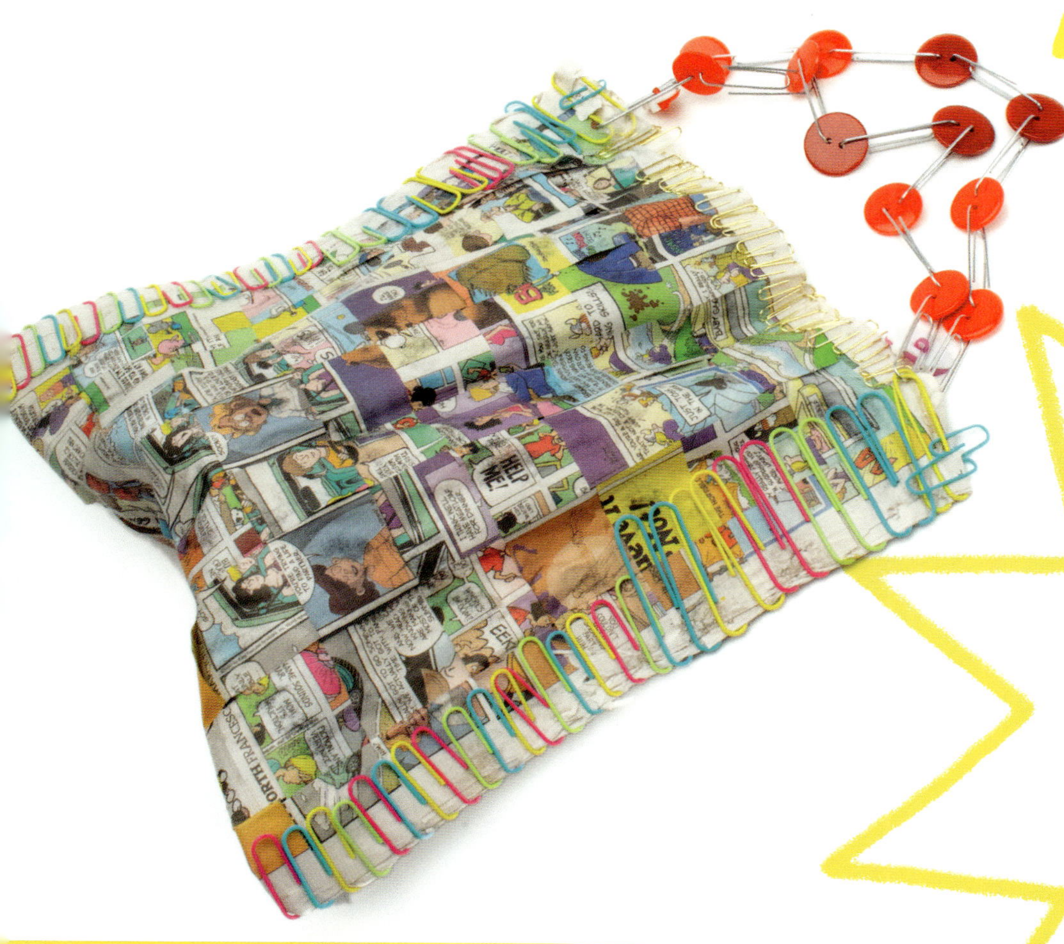

Thread paper clips through button holes to form strong bag handles.

Problem-Solve

Every problem has more than one solution. Is your newspaper bag not sturdy enough? You could fold newspaper into layered strips before weaving them into a bag. Or you could turn your bag upside down into a silly hat!

Your Turn!

Could you weave strips of newspaper into a vest?

How could you make buttons into backpack pins?

Could you connect many paper clips into a belt?

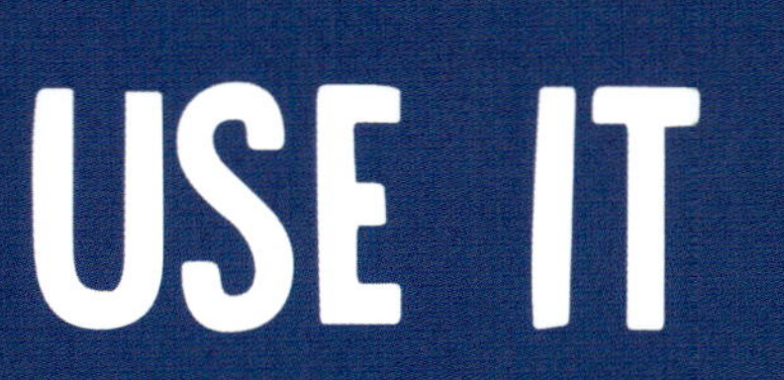

USE IT

Think of an item you need. Then **design** it! Newspaper, buttons, and paper clips provide many options for functional projects.

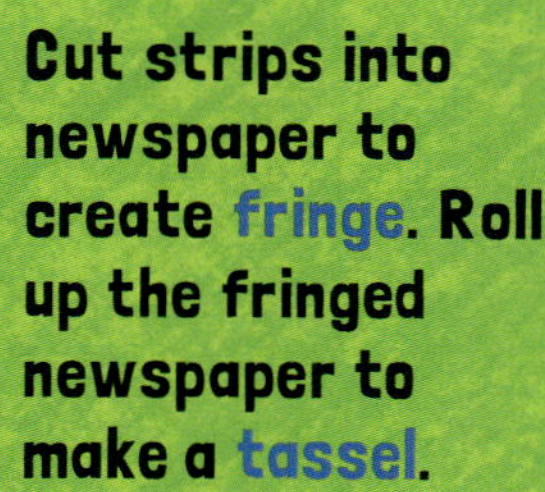

Cut strips into newspaper to create fringe. Roll up the fringed newspaper to make a tassel.

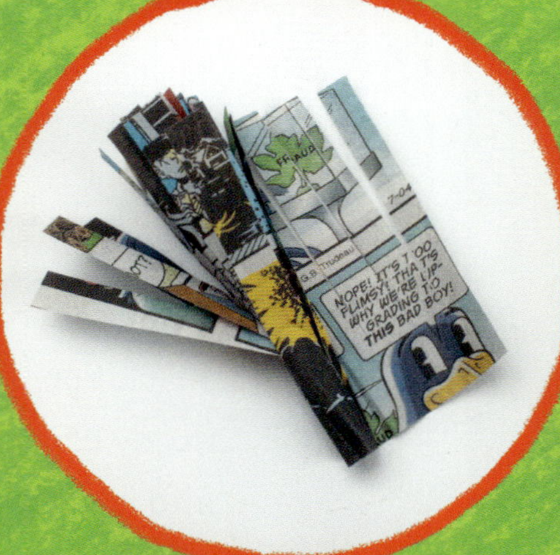

Thread the paper clip through the loop of a decorative button.

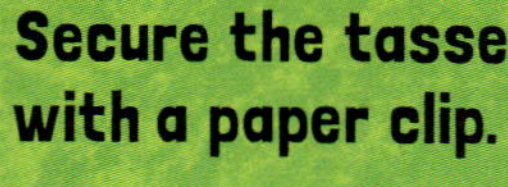

Secure the tassel with a paper clip.

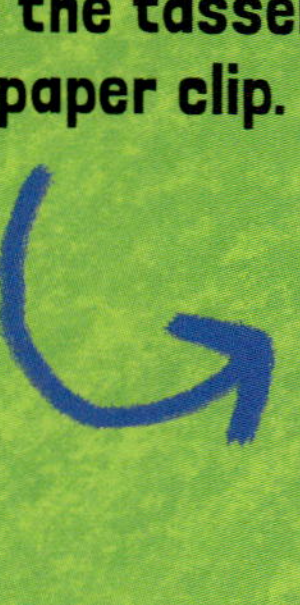

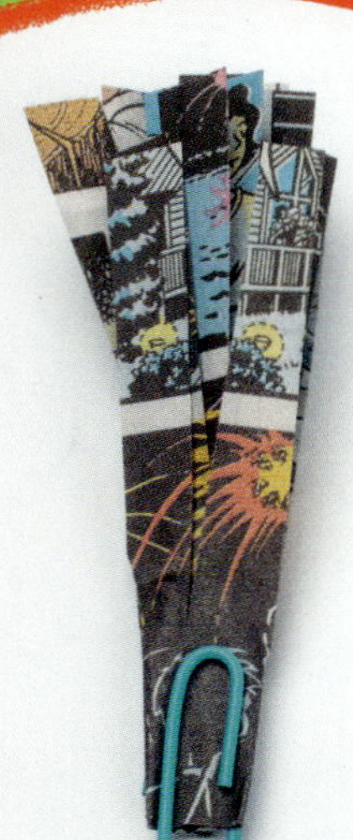

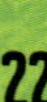

Use your newspaper tassels as bookmarks. You could also attach magnets to the tassels and hang them on your refrigerator or locker door!

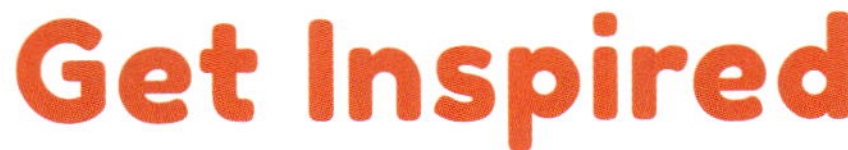

Get Inspired

Think about items you use every day, such as pillows or hair clips. Look at these functional items as you come up with your own designs.

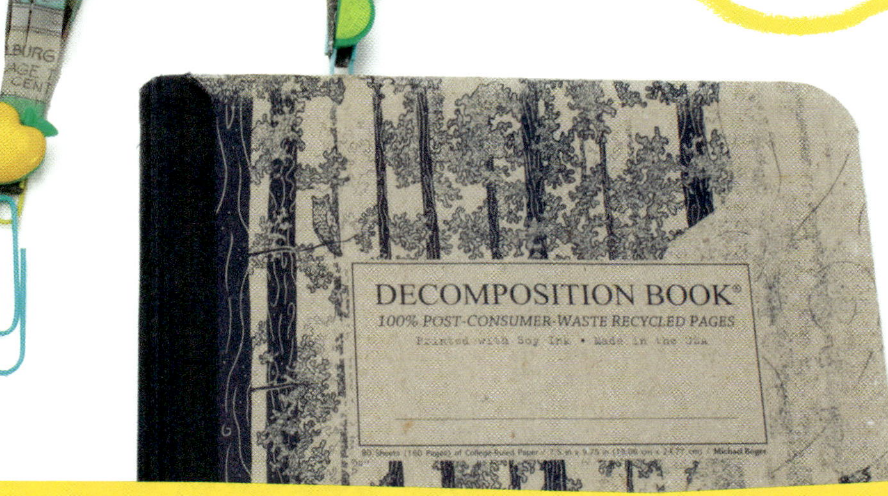

Your Turn!

Could you use strips of newspaper as padding in a camp pillow?

Could you make name tags out of large buttons?

How might you create a bag using only paper clips?

BUILD IT

Engineers use all kinds of materials to build. What do you want to construct? Can you do it using only newspaper, buttons, and paper clips?

Fold a sheet of newspaper into a strip about 1 inch (2.5 cm) wide. Tightly roll up the strip and secure it with a paper clip.

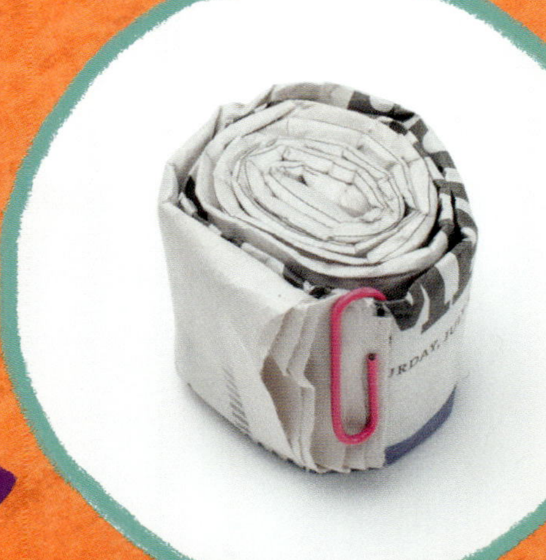

Add more folded newspaper strips and paper clips to your roll to make a large, solid base.

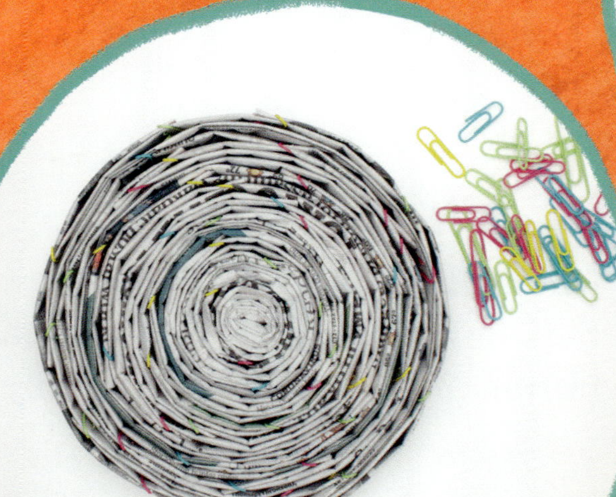

Pull the outer layers of the newspaper roll upward to form a bowl!

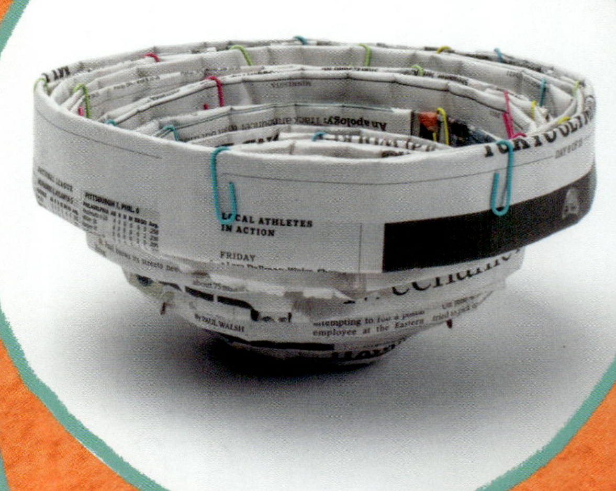

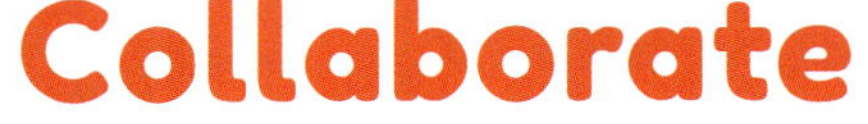

Collaborate

Don't be afraid to ask a friend or classmate for help with your project. Other makers might have ideas you didn't think of! They can also lend a hand during construction.

Decorate the rim of your bowl with buttons.

Your Turn!

How would you make a stool or chair out of rolled up newspaper?

How might you use buttons when building a fairy hut?

Could you use paper clips to build bridges or ladders?

GIFT IT

Is a holiday or birthday coming up? Do you want to surprise a friend or family member just for fun? You can make all kinds of homemade gifts using newspaper, buttons, and paper clips.

Cut newspaper into strips and wind them around a paper clip to make beads. Use a dab of glue at the beginning and end of the strip.

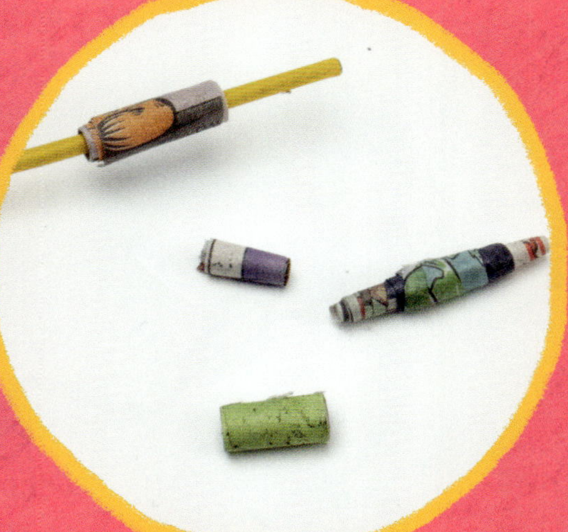

You can thread a paper clip through the loop on the back of a button.

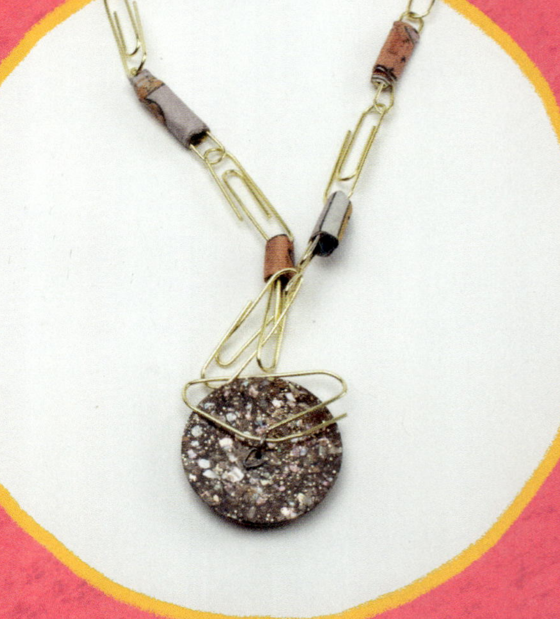

Push paper clips through the newspaper beads. Connect the paper clips to form a chain.

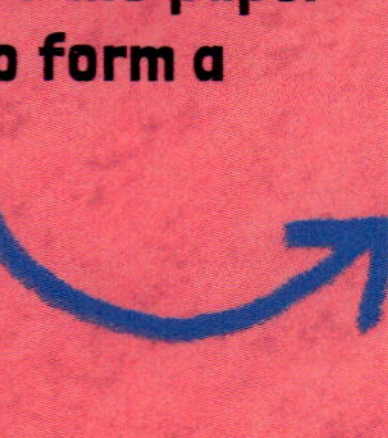

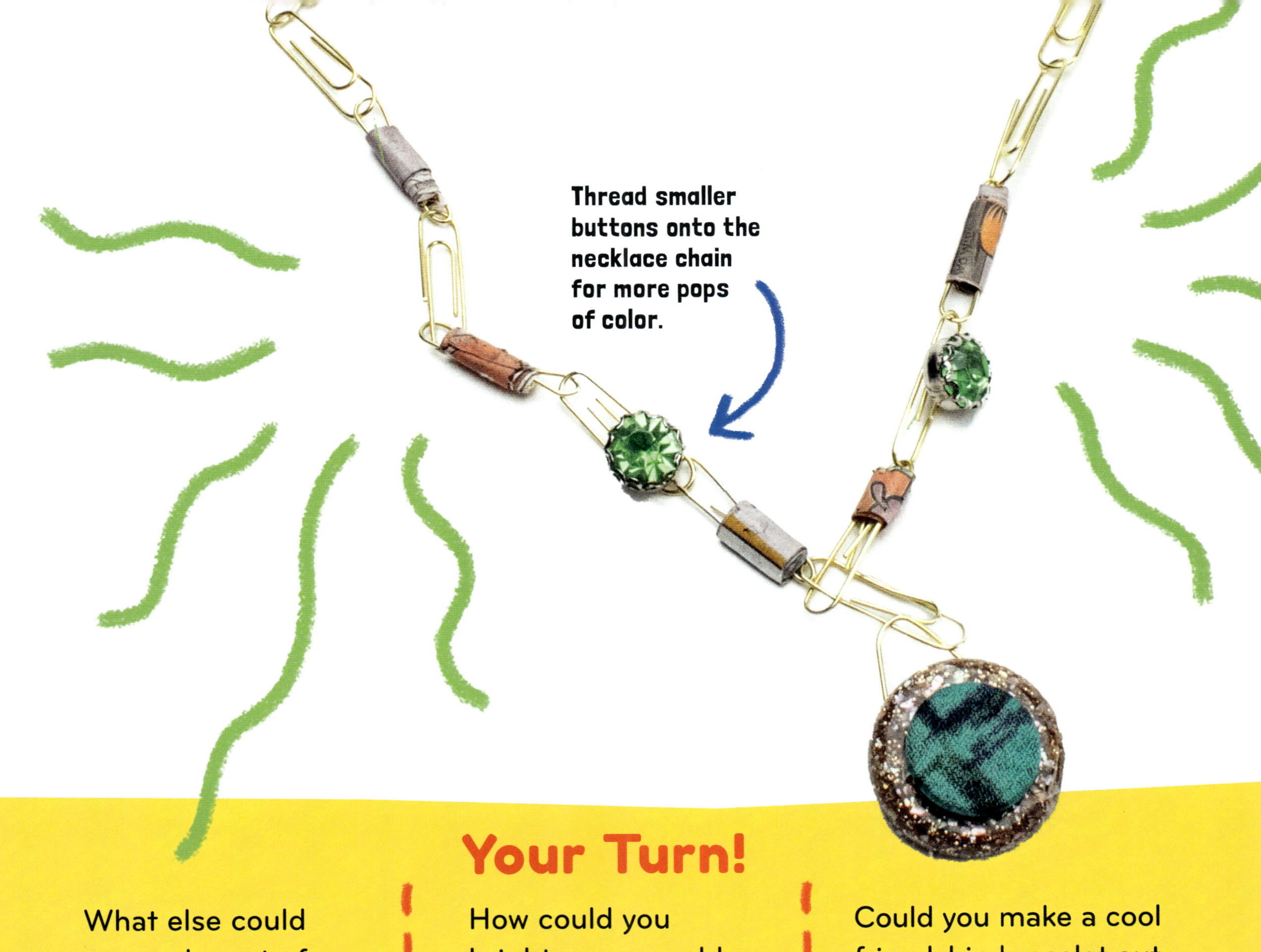

Your Turn!

What else could you make out of newspaper beads?

How could you brighten up an old photo frame using buttons?

Could you make a cool friendship bracelet out of different sizes of paper clips?

PLAY WITH IT

Looking for something fun to do? Use newspaper, buttons, and paper clips to create your own toys and games!

A single sheet of newspaper makes a great **parachute**! Watercolors give it light color without drying stiff.

Newspaper strips become strong string when twisted. Tie the strings to the corner paper clips.

Secure paper clips to the four corners of your parachute.

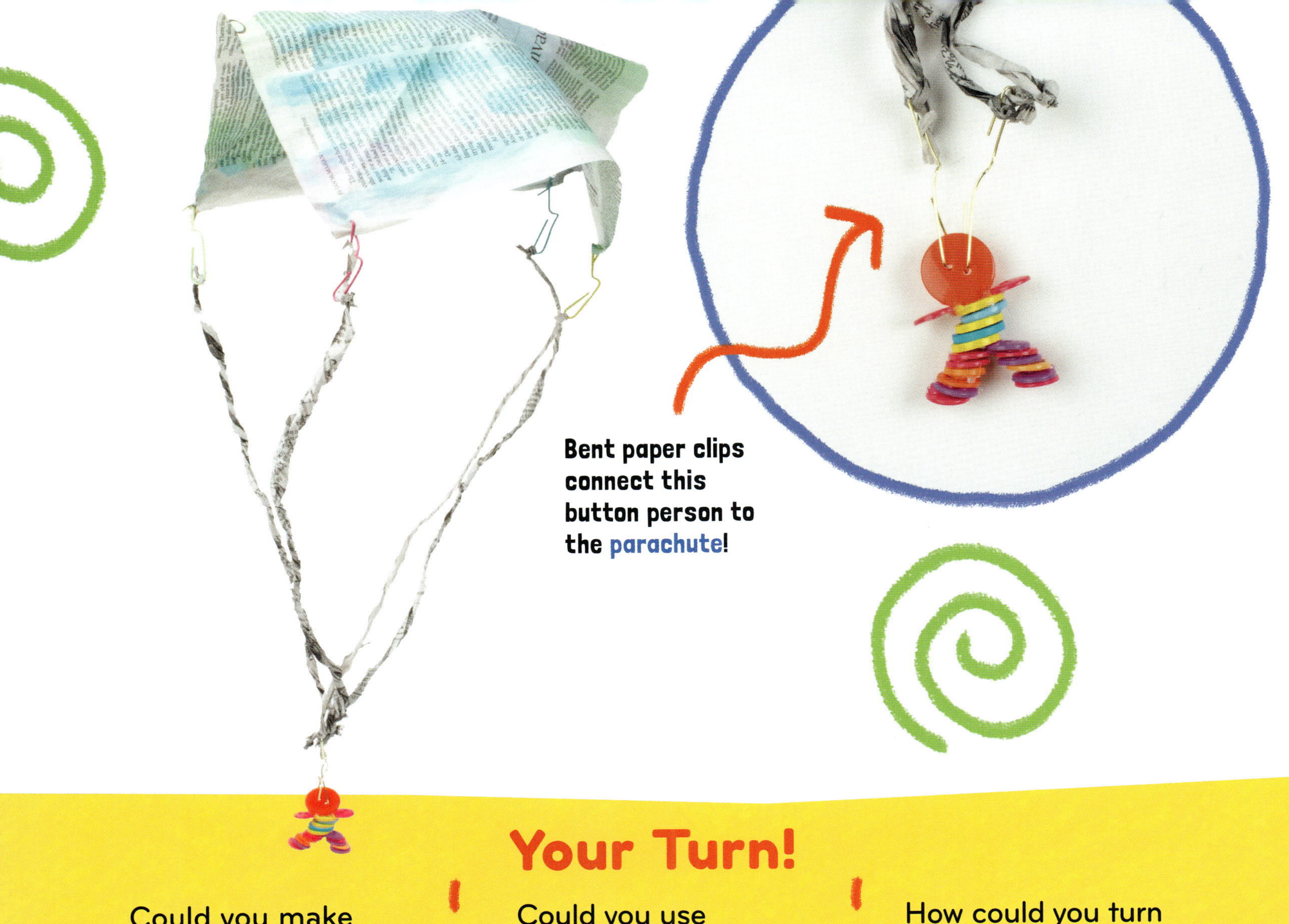

Bent paper clips connect this button person to the **parachute**!

Your Turn!

Could you make drumsticks out of tightly rolled newspaper?

Could you use buttons to create a score keeper?

How could you turn paper clips into mini superheroes?

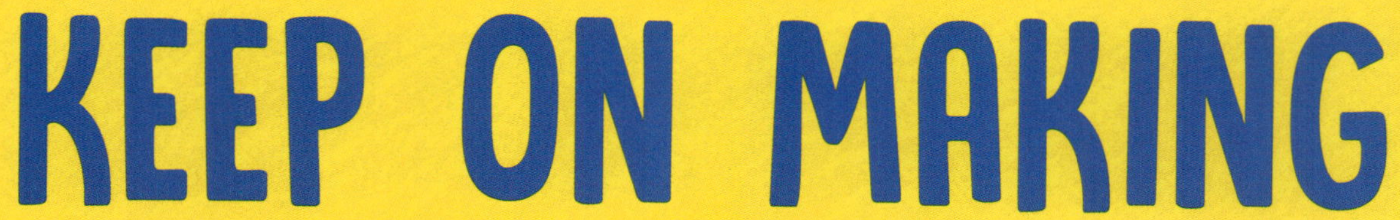

KEEP ON MAKING

Your newspaper, button, and paper clip projects may look complete, but don't close your makerspace toolbox yet. Think about what would make these projects even better. What would you do differently if you made each one again? What would happen if you used different methods or added another material?

Beyond the Makerspace

You can use your makerspace toolbox beyond the makerspace! You might use it to accomplish everyday tasks, such as mending a pair of jeans or building a fort. But makers use the same toolbox to do big things. One day, these tools could help create a new fashion trend or help humans live longer. Turn your world into a makerspace! What problems could you solve?

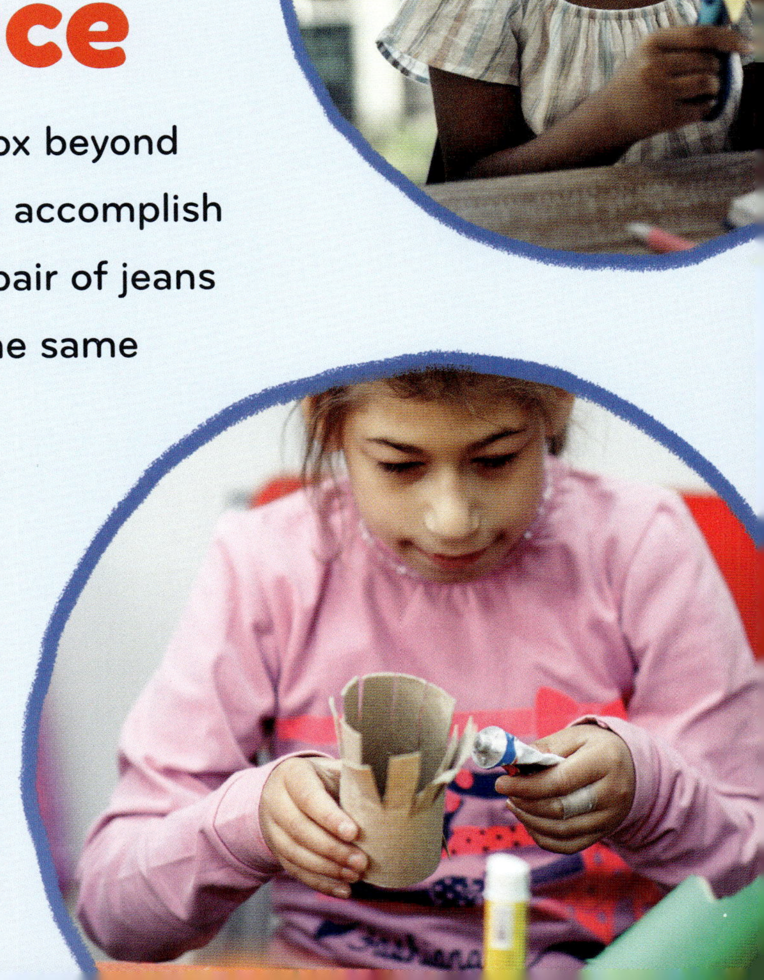

GLOSSARY

accessory – a piece of jewelry or clothing that makes an outfit appear more complete.

canvas – a piece of cloth or other material on which an artist paints.

collaboration – the act of working with others.

design – to plan how something will appear or work. A design is a sketch or outline of something that will be made.

detail – a small part of something.

durable – long lasting and able to withstand wear.

fabric – woven material or cloth.

fringe – a border made up of hanging strips or threads.

parachute – a large piece of cloth used to slow a fall through air.

prop – to support by placing something under or against.

pulp – a soft, moist material prepared from various fibers, such as wood.

solution – an answer to, or a way to solve, a problem.

tassel – a decoration made by gathering loose threads or cords and tying them at one end.